7.19

D1213079

RACE
AND
SPORTS

FIGHTING STEREOTYPES IN SPORTS

BY DUCHESS HARRIS, JD, PHD
WITH CARLA MOONEY

Essential Library

An Imprint of Abdo Publishing | abdobooks.com

ABDOBOOKS.COM

Published by Abdo Publishing, a division of ABDO, PO Box 398166, Minneapolis, Minnesota 55439. Copyright © 2019 by Abdo Consulting Group, Inc. International copyrights reserved in all countries. No part of this book may be reproduced in any form without written permission from the publisher. Essential Library™ is a trademark and logo of Abdo Publishing.

Printed in the United States of America, North Mankato, Minnesota
092018
012019

THIS BOOK CONTAINS
RECYCLED MATERIALS

Cover Photo: Liu Zishan/Shutterstock Images
Interior Photos: Martin Meissner/AP Images, 4–5; Sean Kilpatrick/The Canadian Press/AP Images, 7; Peter Morgan/AP Images, 10; AP Images, 15, 17, 23; New York Daily News Archive/Getty Images, 21; Marty Lederhandler/AP Images, 25; Gerry Broome/AP Images, 29; Lenny Ignelzi/AP Images, 32; Alex Brandon/AP Images, 34; Damian Strohmeyer/AP Images, 36; David J. Phillip/AP Images, 41; Tetsu Joko/Yomiuri Shimbun/AP Images, 43; Jerry Larson/AP Images, 47; Kathy Willens/AP Images, 49; John Crouch/Cal Sport Media/AP Images, 55; John Woods/The Canadian Press/AP Images, 57; Chris Szagola/Cal Sport Media/AP Images, 64; Brandon Dill/AP Images, 63; Julian C. Wilson/AP Images, 67; Tony Dejak/AP Images, 69, 80–81; Carolyn Kaster/AP Images, 73; Mark Cowan/AP Images, 76; Shutterstock Images, 83; Amy Sancetta/AP Images, 88; Charles Rex Arbogast/AP Images, 90–91; Sergey Ponomarev/AP Images, 95; Gene J. Puskar/AP Images, 99

Editor: Patrick Donnelly
Series Designer: Craig Hinton

LIBRARY OF CONGRESS CONTROL NUMBER: 2018947971

PUBLISHER'S CATALOGING-IN-PUBLICATION DATA

Names: Harris, Duchess, author. | Mooney, Carla, author.
Title: Fighting stereotypes in sports / by Duchess Harris and Carla Mooney.
Description: Minneapolis, Minnesota : Abdo Publishing, 2019 | Series: Race and sports | Includes online resources and index.
Identifiers: ISBN 9781532116698 (lib. bdg.) | ISBN 9781532159534 (ebook)
Subjects: LCSH: Stereotypes (Social psychology)--Juvenile literature. | Stereotypes (Social psychology) in sports--Juvenile literature. | Racism in sports--Juvenile literature. | Race relations--Juvenile literature.
Classification: DDC 796.089--dc23

CONTENTS

A HISTORIC FIRST

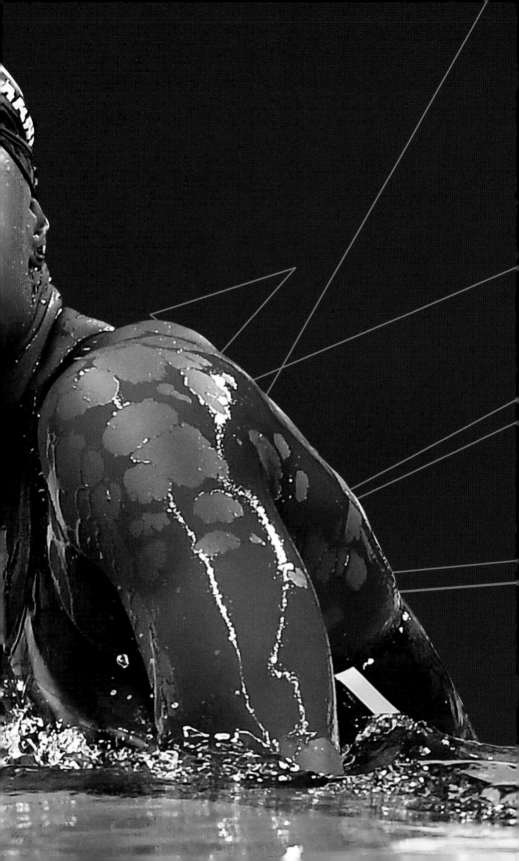

American swimmer Simone Manuel stood on the starting blocks before the finals of the women's 100-meter freestyle race at the 2016 Olympic Games in Rio de Janeiro, Brazil. The reigning world champion, Bronte Campbell from Australia, stood on her right. On her left was Bronte's sister Cate Campbell, who held the world record in the race. Yet Manuel was not intimidated. When the starting buzzer sounded, she dove into the pool and swam fearlessly.

The 100-meter freestyle race is a furious dash for two lengths of the pool. A fraction of a second can be the difference between winning a medal or going home empty handed. This time, Manuel did not have her best start. At the turn, she trailed the leaders by almost a half second. She swam fiercely down the final length of the pool, inching closer to the lead with each stroke.

With her head down for the final 15 meters, Manuel charged and stretched to get her hand on the wall first. When she turned to look at the scoreboard, her jaw dropped. She had tied for first with Canadian Penny Oleksiak and swam an Olympic-record time of 52.70 seconds. In the historic race, Manuel also became the first African American woman to win an individual Olympic gold medal in swimming. She was not finished in Rio,

Manuel and Penny Oleksiak pose with their gold medals.

later earning a silver medal with her teammates in the 4x100-meter freestyle relay.

After receiving her gold medal, Manuel acknowledged the historic impact of her victory. The 20-year-old Stanford University student from Sugar Land, Texas, thanked trailblazing black swimmers such as Cullen Jones and Maritza Correia. "The gold medal wasn't just for me. It was for people who came before me and inspired me to stay in the sport," Manuel said. "And for people who believe that they can't do it. I hope that I'm an inspiration to others to get out there and try swimming."[1]

OVERCOMING FEAR AND ENCOURAGING DIVERSITY

Manuel's high-profile accomplishments may be an inspiration for other people of color to encourage them to try the sport of swimming, which has historically lacked diversity. Miriam Lynch from Diversity in Aquatics, a nonprofit organization that works to reduce the high number of drowning deaths for African Americans, said that Manuel's golden victory could help reverse a long-standing fear of swimming in the black community. The fear is linked to slavery and Jim Crow laws that segregated swimming and kept black swimmers out of white pools. Many years after the end of segregated pools, black swimmers still lag behind their white peers. According to a report commissioned by USA Swimming, if a parent does not swim, there is only a 13 percent chance their child will learn to swim. The report also found that 69 percent of black children and 58 percent of Latino children are unable to swim, compared with 42 percent of white children.[2]

Not being able to swim can put children at greater risk of drowning. Black children are almost three times as likely to drown as white children.[3] Lynch hopes

ERVIN BREAKS THROUGH

In 2000, Anthony Ervin became the first swimmer of African heritage to earn a spot on the US Olympic team. He was also the first to medal, winning gold in the men's 50-meter freestyle and silver in the 4x100-meter freestyle relay at that year's Games in Sydney, Australia. Ervin retired from swimming in 2003 and spent several years traveling the world. However, his love of swimming drew him back to the sport. He competed for Team USA in both the 2012 London and 2016 Rio Olympics. In Rio, Ervin returned to top form, winning the gold medal in the 50-meter freestyle race.

that Manuel's success will inspire young children of color to try swimming. "When you see that the lifeguard is from the community, you think, 'I can be a lifeguard; I can be a coach,'" Lynch said. "Now, with Simone, it's 'I can be an Olympian.'"[4]

BREAKING STEREOTYPES

Manuel's win in the pool was also a victory over long-held stereotypes that African Americans are poor swimmers. In Manuel's family, basketball was the sport of choice—her two older brothers and father played basketball in college. However, basketball never quite clicked for her. Instead, Manuel thrived in the pool. She had originally learned how to swim at age four so she could be safe in the water. Once in the pool, her talent was unmistakable. In high school, Manuel set national age-group records in both the 50- and 100-meter freestyle events.

Still, being one of the few African Americans in swimming was hard. There were times when Manuel wanted to quit swimming because no one else at the pool looked like her, but her parents and coaches encouraged her to keep training. After her high school graduation in 2014, Manuel went to Stanford, where she set school records and won national titles in the 50- and 100-meter freestyle events. She even beat Missy Franklin, who won multiple

Manuel spent much of her time in Rio talking about her experiences and challenges as a black swimmer.

gold medals at the 2012 Olympic Games, in a 100-meter race held at the Grand Prix in Santa Clara, California.

Manuel recognizes that her success in the pool is helping to break down negative stereotypes related to African Americans and swimming. However, she admits that she does feel the pressure of racing for an entire community on her shoulders. In interviews before her Olympic races, Manuel noted she was asked repeatedly about being a "black swimmer" to the point where it threatened to become a distraction. "That's something I definitely struggled with a lot," Manuel said after winning her gold medal. "Just coming into this race tonight I kind of tried to take the weight of the black community off my shoulders, which is something I carry with me."[5]

Manuel hopes to inspire other swimmers and encourage more athletes of color to enter the sport. "I would like there to be a day where there are more of us, and it's not 'Simone, the black swimmer.' The title 'black swimmer' makes it seem like I'm not supposed to be able to win a gold medal, or I'm not supposed to be able to break records. And that's not true," she said.[6]

WHAT IS A STEREOTYPE?

For Manuel and many other athletes, dealing with stereotypes can be difficult. A stereotype is a fixed, generalized belief about a specific group of people. From stereotypes like "blondes have more fun" to "white men can't jump," these beliefs affect how people see others. A stereotype is like a shortcut for the brain, allowing it to make a quick judgment based on visible characteristics such as race, gender, or age.

Stereotypes are generally based on biases. A bias is a tendency or prejudice toward or against something

PIONEERING TEAMMATE

Before Simone Manuel, Lia Neal was breaking stereotypes in the pool. Neal is the daughter of a Chinese American mother and an African American father. She was the first African American woman to swim in an Olympic final for Team USA, winning a bronze medal in the women's 4x100-meter freestyle race in 2012. She also won a silver medal at the 2016 Rio Olympics in the same event with her American teammates, including Simone Manuel.

HOW DO RACIAL STEREOTYPES FORM?

Stereotypes about race have many roots. The world is a complex place. In order to make sense of the world, it is human nature to sort information into categories. Organizing information into categories makes it simpler and easier to understand. From a young age, people learn to put the people and objects they encounter into categories, including racial categories. Researchers have found that once people categorize someone into a group, they tend to minimize the differences between people in the same group. They also exaggerate the differences between two separate groups. This type of thinking strengthens stereotypes, making it more likely for a person to attribute the same characteristics to all members of a group. Over time, these categories can be influenced and reinforced by parents, peers, and the media and affect how a person labels these categories— either positively or negatively. In addition, the less contact people have with a specific racial group, the more likely they will be to assign negative labels to that group. If someone has a negative experience with a person of another group, it can strengthen any prior negative stereotypes.

or someone. Biases can be based on both positive and negative stereotypes instead of on specific information about a person or circumstance. Some biases are good, such as a bias toward choosing healthy foods to eat. Other biases can be harmful and lead to unfair discrimination. Unfair biases are often based on stereotypes about a person's race, ethnicity, gender, religion, or other characteristic.

That's where stereotypes can cause problems. They cause people to ignore the differences between specific individuals and make generalizations that may not be true about people, simply because they belong to a certain gender, race, class, or other group. This can lead to unfair judgments about individual people.

In the sports world, stereotypes affect athletes of different races and genders. For example, the idea that black people can't swim or that Asian people are not good athletes are negative stereotypes. Problems surface when people believe that stereotypes are true in all cases and use them to put expectations and limitations on athletes. Imagine if a National Football League (NFL) coach believed that white quarterbacks were superior to black quarterbacks. He might pass up drafting Cam Newton or Russell Wilson—both star NFL quarterbacks—simply because of their race. In this way, stereotypes and bias can unfairly and sometimes unintentionally take opportunities away from talented athletes of different racial and ethnic backgrounds. Some of these long-held stereotypes are starting to fade away, but many have been part of the sports world long enough that it's extremely difficult to completely eradicate them.

DISCUSSION STARTERS

- How does Simone Manuel's success influence young swimmers of color?
- What is a common stereotype held about players in your favorite sport?
- Have you ever been harmed by a stereotype? How?

CHAPTER
TWO

HISTORY OF
RACE AND
SPORTS

Stereotypes affect the lives of athletes today, but they're not a new phenomenon. In fact, the prejudices that often stem from stereotyping were a major factor in shaping the sporting landscape in the United States.

In the late 1800s and early 1900s, African American athletes were banned from most professional sports. In response, the black athletic community formed its own teams, leagues, and competitions. The Negro Leagues showcased some of the most talented players in the baseball world. The United Golfers' Association was an advocate for black people who played golf. And in basketball, the New York Renaissance and the Harlem Globetrotters traveled the country entertaining fans with their skill and showmanship.

However, negative stereotypes about black people also grew during segregation. One key factor in breaking down mistaken racial stereotypes is first-hand exposure to people of other races. Segregation kept the races separated, allowing ignorant sentiments and assumptions about black people to take root among whites.

The Pittsburgh Crawfords, 1935 Negro National League champions, pose in front of their team bus.

BASEBALL'S NEGRO LEAGUES

One of the most famous African American leagues in the early 1900s was baseball's Negro Leagues. When black baseball players were forced off white teams, groups of players formed their own teams. From early spring to late fall, these teams traveled around the country, challenging local clubs in small towns and rural areas. They played black or white teams, on sandlots or in major league stadiums. By the end of the 1800s, all-black baseball teams were commonplace.

Between 1900 and 1920, many teams that made the Negro Leagues famous were formed. These included the Chicago American Giants, the New York Lincoln Giants, and the Homestead Grays. Rivalries between the teams were intense. By the end of World War I (1914–1918), baseball was a popular entertainment attraction for urban black populations across the country. In 1920, Andrew "Rube" Foster, the manager of the Chicago American Giants, proposed a national association for the all-black baseball clubs. In Kansas City, Missouri, Foster and the owners of the top black teams met and formed the Negro National League. Led by Foster, the league continued for most of the

1920s. It fell victim to the Great Depression and dissolved after the 1931 season.

After Foster's Negro National League folded, a tavern owner from Pittsburgh named Gus Greenlee put together a second version of the league in 1933. Greenlee's Negro National League was a hit. Two other leagues, the Negro Southern League and the Negro American League, also provided opportunities for black baseball players.

Despite the economic downturn after the Great Depression, the three major Negro leagues prospered. The leagues had solid financing throughout the 1930s and early 1940s, with most clubs at least breaking even. Negro League annual revenues climbed to $2 million during World War II (1939–1945).[1] The Negro Leagues were one of the biggest and most successful organizations run by black business owners in the United States. Black Americans proved that they didn't need the permission or support of white Americans to participate in professional sports.

TRAILBLAZERS PARTICIPATING IN WHITE SPORTS

Although most black athletes competed separately from white athletes during the early 1900s, some successfully participated in predominantly white sports. Athletes such as Jack Johnson, Joe Louis, and Jesse Owens competed against whites in individual sports such as boxing and track.

Born in 1878 in Texas, Johnson began boxing as a teenager. At the time, black boxers could compete for some titles but not for the world heavyweight championship. Johnson boxed and built his reputation and wealth by winning matches against black fighters and white fighters. Looking to face the best in the world, Johnson repeatedly challenged James J. Jeffries, the white heavyweight champion, to a match. However, Jeffries refused to fight a black man. Instead, he retired undefeated in 1904.

Four years later, Johnson's chance to fight for the title arrived when the new heavyweight champion, Tommy Burns, agreed to face him. In a match in Australia, Johnson beat Burns to become the first African American heavyweight champion of the world. Despite his athletic success, the racism embedded in many white Americans prevented them from accepting Johnson as a champion. Twenty years later, a different black boxer would be more widely embraced by all Americans, regardless of race.

Joseph Louis Barrow—who would come to be known by his first two names, Joe Louis—was born in Alabama in 1914. A schoolmate suggested he take up boxing, and Louis took it from there. He won 50 of his 54 amateur fights. Then in 1934 Louis turned pro. He began his professional career with 27 consecutive victories, including 23 by knockout. Finally, German boxer Max Schmeling beat Louis in 1936. But Louis got back in the ring, knocking out James Braddock

Joe Louis reads all about his first-round knockout of Max Schmeling the day after their 1938 rematch.

in 1937 to win the world heavyweight title. Louis was a hero to the black community. One year later, a rematch against Schmeling made Louis a hero to all Americans.

In the 1930s, Adolf Hitler and the Nazi Party rose to power in Germany, threatening world peace. Schmeling was widely viewed as a symbol of Hitler and the Nazis. Meanwhile, Louis represented the United States and democracy. The boxers squared off before 70,000 fans at Yankee Stadium in New York City. It wasn't even close. "The Brown Bomber" knocked out Schmeling in the first round. That made Louis a hero that all Americans could celebrate.

In 1936, another young black athlete won over white fans by demonstrating American greatness in the face of Nazi arrogance. One year earlier, Ohio State University's Jesse Owens had dominated the Big Ten Conference track-and-field meet, setting four world records in a span of 45 minutes. Then he set his sights on the Olympics. In 1936, the Games were held in Berlin, Germany. Hitler viewed it as a chance for Germany's white athletes to demonstrate their racial superiority. It didn't quite work out that way.

Owens swept the 100- and 200-meter races, took gold in the long jump, and ran the opening leg as the US team cruised to victory in the 4x100-relay. He became the first American track-and-field athlete to win four gold medals in a single Olympics. Owens, like Louis, brought Americans together, allowing them to—at least briefly—overlook their

Jesse Owens received a hero's welcome in Cleveland, Ohio, when he returned from the 1936 Olympics in Berlin, Germany.

own racial prejudices and cheer black athletes on to victory against Hitler and Germany.

At the end of World War II (1939–1945), the movement to fully integrate American sports gained strength. African Americans had fought for their country—had died for their country—in the war zones of Europe and Asia. Back home, more and more Americans believed they also should be able to play professional sports as well.

SHATTERING BASEBALL'S COLOR LINE

On April 15, 1947, Jackie Robinson started at first base for the Brooklyn Dodgers, breaking the Major League Baseball (MLB) color line. But what has become one of the most famous examples of successful racial integration was not universally accepted at first. Many white fans and players did not want Robinson playing against white men. Some of his own teammates were unhappy about having Robinson in their locker room. Opponents harassed him, throwing pitches at his head, spitting on his shoes, and spiking him with their cleats. Fans were ruthless with their insults. Anonymous death threats and hate letters even reached Robinson and his family.

But some important people were in Robinson's corner, and they let everyone else know it. All-Star shortstop Pee Wee Reese was among Robinson's most vocal supporters. So were MLB Commissioner Happy Chandler, National League (NL) President Ford Frick, and retired slugger Hank Greenberg, a Jewish ballplayer who faced similar prejudices when he starred for the Detroit Tigers in the 1930s and 1940s. When some of Robinson's teammates grumbled about playing with him, Dodgers general manager Branch Rickey said that he would trade them before he traded Robinson.

Through it all, Robinson held his temper and maintained his dignity, allowing his talent to speak for itself. He won the MLB Rookie of the Year Award in his first year with the Dodgers, hitting 12 home runs and leading the NL with 29 stolen bases as Brooklyn captured the NL pennant. Two years later, Robinson posted a league-leading .342 batting average and stole 37 bases en route to winning the NL Most Valuable Player (MVP) Award.

Jackie Robinson holds the trophy he received for winning the 1949 National League MVP Award.

The Dodgers won the NL pennant six times in Robinson's 10 seasons in Brooklyn, with the highlight coming in 1955, when they won the ultimate prize, defeating the New York Yankees to win the World Series. Robinson's fielding, base running, and consistent hitting played a key role in all of Brooklyn's success.

Robinson retired in 1957 with a career batting average of .311 and 197 stolen bases. He also stole home a record 19 times in his career. Five years later, in his first year of eligibility, Robinson was voted into the Baseball Hall of Fame. His success provided opportunities to other black

THE CIVIL RIGHTS MOVEMENT BEGINS

While color lines were cracking in professional sports, black people in the 1950s were becoming more vocal for change. Black papers and communities called for equal voting rights. They wanted access to the same public places as whites. Black people wanted their children to have the same education as whites. They also wanted the same opportunities in employment and housing.

A major step toward civil rights occurred in 1953, when the Supreme Court ruled in *Terry v. Adams* that black people be allowed to vote in primaries and all elections. The following year, on May 17, 1954, the Supreme Court issued a landmark decision in *Brown v. Board of Education of Topeka, Kansas*. In the decision, the court banned segregation of schools by race. This decision sent shockwaves across the country and angered many southern whites. Tensions came to a head in 1957 in Little Rock, Arkansas. When officials tried to integrate the school, they met resistance from white mobs and government officials. Images of the violence in Little Rock swept through newspapers and television. Eventually, President Dwight Eisenhower sent the Arkansas National Guard to Little Rock to take control and calm the situation. Although the crisis in Little Rock was resolved, the civil rights movement was just beginning.

players, as MLB rosters became more diverse throughout the 1950s. It also gave white Americans the opportunity to see black athletes not only succeeding on the field, but also justly claiming their rights as US citizens.

TAKING THE FIELD

After Robinson's debut, college and professional sports became increasingly integrated. According to a 2017 report by the Institute for Diversity and Ethics in Sport at the University of Central Florida, in Division I college athletics,

African Americans represent 44.2 percent of football players and 53.0 percent of basketball players.[2] In addition, college football's most coveted individual honor, the Heisman Trophy, was awarded to African American players five times between 2010 and 2016.

In the major professional leagues, more African American athletes are taking the field than ever before. According to the Institute for Diversity and Ethics in Sport, African American athletes made up 69.7 percent of NFL players in 2016. In the National Basketball Association (NBA) during the 2016–17 season, 80.9 percent of players identified as people of color. In MLB, 42.5 percent of players were people of color at the start of the 2017 season.[3] With more opportunities to play, athletes of all races and ethnicities have risen to the top of their sports. Yet even though sports have made great strides in diversity and integration, stereotypes and bias still exist.

DISCUSSION STARTERS

- Do you think the history of segregation in sports has contributed to sports stereotypes today? Why or why not?
- What impact did sports and trailblazing athletes have on American society?
- How did the civil rights movement affect athletes?

CHAPTER THREE

ATHLETIC OR INTELLIGENT?

Although many sports have made great strides in integrating athletes of color, racial stereotypes still exist. One of the most common racial stereotypes—that black athletes succeed because of physical skills and natural athleticism, while white athletes rely on hard work, discipline, and intelligence—has persisted for years.

REVEALING WORDS

Leading up to the fortieth anniversary of Jackie Robinson's entry into major league baseball in 1987, Los Angeles Dodgers vice president Al Campanis appeared on ABC's *Nightline*, a television show hosted by journalist Ted Koppel. During the interview, Koppel asked Campanis, who had been Robinson's teammate and roommate in the minor leagues, why 40 years after the color barrier had been broken, there were still so few black people in baseball's management positions. Campanis replied, "I truly believe that they may not have some of the necessities to be, let's say, a field manager, or perhaps a general manager."[1]

Later in the interview, Campanis talked about black athletes, saying, "They are gifted with great musculature and various other things, they're fleet of foot, and this is why there are a lot of black major league ballplayers. Now, as far as having the background to become club presidents, or presidents of a bank, I don't know. But I do know when I look at a black ballplayer, I am looking at him physically and whether he has the mental approach to play in the big leagues."[2]

Campanis's comments caused an uproar, and within 48 hours of the interview, the Dodgers forced him to resign. The comments also caused some people to ask why in MLB, where more than 25 percent of players were black, there had been only three black managers. When asked about Campanis's comments, Frank Robinson, MLB's first black manager, said that he was not surprised. "Baseball has been hiding this ugly prejudice for years—that blacks aren't smart enough to be managers or third-base coaches or part of the front office," said Robinson, who was hired to manage the Cleveland Indians in 1975. "There's a belief that they're fine when it comes to the

SCHOLAR, ATHLETE

Former NFL player Myron Rolle is much more than an African American athlete. While in his senior year at Florida State University, Rolle was awarded a Rhodes Scholarship, a prestigious honor given to only 32 American students annually. After graduation, he deferred his entry into the NFL for a year to continue his studies at Oxford University in England. He earned a master's degree in medical anthropology. Upon returning to the United States, Rolle played three seasons in the NFL. After retiring from football in 2013, Rolle graduated from medical school and in 2017 started his residency in neurosurgery at Harvard Medical School.

Frank Robinson, right, managed the Cleveland Indians, San Francisco Giants, Baltimore Orioles, Montreal Expos, and Washington Nationals.

physical part of the game, but if it involves brains they just can't handle it."[3]

"TOUGH AS ANYONE"

The racial stereotypes exposed by Campanis's comments on national television extend beyond baseball, affecting athletes in sports from football to basketball. During the 2009 National Collegiate Athletic Association (NCAA) women's basketball tournament, University of Connecticut coach Geno Auriemma argued that it wasn't fair for people to view his team's opponent, Stanford, as lesser athletes simply because they were white.

"White kids are always looked upon as being soft. So Stanford's got a tremendous amount of really good players who for whatever reason, because they don't look like [University of Connecticut players] Tina Charles or Maya Moore, the perception out there is going to be, well, they must be soft," Auriemma said. "I watched them play and nobody goes harder to the boards. Nobody takes more charges. Nobody runs the floor as hard. Those kids are as tough as any of the kids in the country. But people in the sports world like to make judgments on people by how they look. And it's grossly unfair," he said.[4] At the same time, the coach insisted that his players—who were mostly African American—should be given credit for their work ethic and discipline, not just physical skills.

RACIAL STEREOTYPES AND QUARTERBACKS

In football, the quarterback is often viewed as the team leader, the player who receives praise for victories and blame for losses. However, for many years, racial stereotypes led people in football to believe that black athletes were not smart enough to play quarterback or lead a team. Following this stereotype, many coaches and team leaders steered talented black quarterbacks who were successful in high school and college into other positions when they entered the NFL.

Warren Moon is a Hall of Fame quarterback who played professional football in the NFL and Canadian Football League (CFL) for 23 seasons. Growing up in Los Angeles,

Connecticut center Tina Charles receives instructions from coach Geno Auriemma.

Moon was a great athlete from an early age. He studied the game and learned different offenses. Yet coaches tried to get him to switch to running back or wide receiver.

"When I was coming out of high school, I was all-city and all-state, and they wanted me to switch to receiver," said Moon, who convinced his coaches to keep him at quarterback.[5] In his senior season at the University of Washington in 1977, Moon led his team to a Rose Bowl victory. NFL scouts, however, told him to try playing wide receiver. "I refused; I will go to Siberia to play quarterback, but I will not switch positions," he said.[6]

Undrafted by an NFL team, Moon signed with the CFL's Edmonton Eskimos. He quarterbacked the team to five consecutive league championships and became the first professional player to pass for 5,000 yards in a single season. In 1984, Moon returned to the United States and joined the NFL's Houston Oilers.

In Houston's wide-open offense, Moon displayed his impressive quarterback skills, highlighting his strong arm and ability to make quick decisions. In 17 seasons in the NFL, Moon threw for nearly 50,000 passing yards and broke numerous records. He was inducted into the Pro Football Hall of Fame in 2006. Yet he admits that the pressure of being a black quarterback was overwhelming at times.

"I felt like I was going out there half the time representing my race as opposed to representing my team and teammates," Moon said. "I wonder how much better I might have been if I'd had more fun."[7]

SUPER BOWL CHAMPION

A few years after Moon's entry into the NFL, another quarterback shattered the racial stereotype that a black quarterback could not be successful. In 1988, Doug Williams led the underdog Washington Redskins to a 42–10 victory over the Denver Broncos in the Super Bowl. In the win, he

Quarterback Warren Moon refused to change positions, a decision that ultimately led him to the Pro Football Hall of Fame.

passed for 340 yards and four touchdowns. Williams not only became the first black quarterback to win a Super Bowl but also was named the game's MVP.

Williams's victory in the NFL's biggest game proved that color did not matter. He showed that black quarterbacks could lead a team, run an offense, and do everything just as well as white quarterbacks. It was a groundbreaking moment for black quarterbacks and black athletes across the league. For future NFL quarterback Rodney Peete, who at the time was a junior at the University of Southern California (USC), watching Williams gave him the confidence that he too could have a chance to be an NFL quarterback. "It was a sight to see; truly amazing. But it was more than that," said Peete. "It didn't have quite the global impact of Jesse Owens going to Berlin and winning the [1936] Olympics, but it was something that was so powerful—something that a lot of people running these [NFL] organizations didn't believe could happen."[8]

PROGRESS MADE BUT BIAS STILL EXISTS

The success of Moon and Williams opened doors for black quarterbacks who came later, such as Donovan McNabb, Russell Wilson, and Cam Newton. For many years, it was rare to see a black quarterback selected in the first round of the NFL draft. In 1999, three of the five quarterbacks selected in the first round of the NFL draft were black—McNabb, Akili Smith, and Daunte Culpepper. Then in 2001, the Atlanta Falcons

THE NBA'S THUGS

In the late 1990s and early 2000s, NBA players began to embrace hip-hop culture, which was on display in the way players dressed, the tattoos they sported, and the way they spoke to the media. Some fans formed negative stereotypes about the players based on the media's presentation of hip-hop, including its focus on glorifying crime. Then in November 2004, a game between the Indiana Pacers and the Detroit Pistons resulted in a bench-clearing brawl. Fans threw objects at players, and the Pacers' Ron Artest went into the stands to confront the fans. The brawl cast a negative light on the NBA and cemented its negative stereotype in the minds of many observers.

selected Michael Vick, a black quarterback, as the overall first pick of the draft. Other black quarterbacks who were chosen with the first pick of the draft include JaMarcus Russell in 2007, Newton in 2011, and Jameis Winston in 2015.

Even though some progress has been made to break down the stereotype of the athletic black athlete versus the smart white athlete, some bias still exists and affects the public's perception of black quarterbacks and athletes. In the NFL, black quarterbacks are more likely to be described by their natural physical abilities and strength. In comparison, white quarterbacks are more likely to be praised for their leadership, intelligence, preparation, and work ethic.

Two studies by Patrick Ferrucci, a researcher at the University of Colorado, suggest that racial bias still influences how the public views quarterbacks. In the first study, researchers asked black and white college students to rate paragraphs and photos of black and white professional quarterbacks using four descriptors: physical strength,

DUMB JOCK STEREOTYPE

Another stereotype—that of the dumb jock—affects athletes of every race and ethnic background. In some cases, it may be a self-fulfilling prophecy. According to research from Stanford University, anxiety over being labeled a "dumb jock" can actually cause some student athletes to perform worse in the classroom, especially if they are male.[9]

natural ability, leadership, and intelligence. They found that while all participants stereotyped the quarterbacks by race, black participants stereotyped both races more strongly, indicating that stereotypes affect how black athletes view themselves and play football from a younger age.

In the second study, the researchers surveyed only white participants from a variety of ages and education levels and asked them to rate the paragraphs and photos. They found that the participants used stereotypes to describe the black quarterbacks, but not the white ones. For example, even when told that both a white and black quarterback were very smart, the white participants did not rate the black player as equally smart as the white player. While the findings reveal the racial stereotypes that still exist on the field, study author Ferrucci believes the results may also impact the world outside of sports. "If we're still stereotyping this way in sports, then it's probable that we're stereotyping in real life, too, and that could have far more negative consequences," Ferrucci said.[10]

DISCUSSION STARTERS

- How do you think stereotypes limit opportunities for people of a particular group?
- Has someone believed a stereotype about you that is not true?
- How can a stereotype that all black athletes are physically gifted lead to racism?

LAMAR JACKSON
DEFIES NFL SCOUTS

Before the 2018 NFL draft, racial stereotypes surfaced in the form of questions about University of Louisville quarterback Lamar Jackson's chance to succeed as an NFL quarterback. Jackson, who became the youngest Heisman Trophy winner in history, is a dual-threat quarterback with the ability to pass and run on any play.

Before the draft, several scouts, including veteran NFL executive Bill Polian, suggested that Jackson switch to wide receiver. They questioned whether his 6-foot-3-inch (191 cm), 212-pound (96 kg) body could hold up as a quarterback in the NFL. At the same time, similar concerns were not mentioned about white quarterbacks in the draft with builds similar to Jackson's.

"It is annoying because quarterback is all I played all my life. People look at my legs and they see I can make big plays, but they don't really see my arm, and I make big plays with my arm," Jackson said in response to scouts who think he should change positions. "I scored more touchdowns with my arm than my legs."[11]

Jackson was selected with the final pick of the first round by the Baltimore Ravens, who expected him to be the team's quarterback of the future.

The Baltimore Ravens put their faith in Lamar Jackson at the 2018 NFL draft.

CHAPTER FOUR

TOO SMALL, TOO SLOW?

Growing up in the Washington, DC, area in the 1990s, Mike Mon became used to the comments he would get as a Chinese American each time he stepped onto a basketball court. "How many times did I hear 'Bruce Lee'?" asked Mon, referring to the famous actor and martial arts expert. "Nonstop. I'm sure a lot of other players got that, too."[1]

Yet basketball had been in Mon's family for generations. Both Mon's father and his grandfather played in Chinese American community basketball leagues. In fact, Asian American basketball leagues have existed in the United States for almost a century and remain popular today. For example, in Southern California, an estimated 14,000 Japanese Americans play in regular club and weekend tournaments.[2] Yet despite the popularity of youth basketball in the Asian American community, few Asian American athletes play Division I college basketball and only a couple have made it as professional players in the NBA.

According to the NCAA, of the 5,472 Division I men's basketball players in the 2015–16 season, only 14 were Asian American. The lack of Asian American athletes in collegiate sports extends beyond basketball. According to the NCAA's statistics, there were only 115 Asian Americans out of 28,380 football players. In baseball, only 89 players out of 10,430 were Asian. For these three sports, Asian Americans made up less than one percent of Division I athletes.[3]

According to Asian American athletes and other experts, the low numbers of Asian Americans in college and pro sports is most likely caused by a combination of factors. To begin, they acknowledge that many Asian American families value education over sports and pressure their kids to focus first on academics. "'Where's basketball going to get you?' 'Where's football going to get you?' 'Your odds of becoming an NBA player are one in a million,'" said Mon, demonstrating the pressure Asian American athletes face from their families. "'But your odds of becoming a doctor. . . . If you study hard, you put the work in, you determine your own fate.' That has a lot to do with it. There are other ways to succeed in life besides athletics."[4]

Yet this pressure to perform academically has

OHNO PILES UP THE MEDALS

Japanese American skater Apolo Ohno is a pioneer in Olympic short track skating. At the 2002 Olympic Winter Games in Salt Lake City, Utah, Ohno won a gold medal in the 1500-meter and a silver in the 1000-meter race. He followed up those wins with a gold and two bronze medals in the 2006 Olympic Winter Games in Turin, Italy, and a silver and two bronze medals in the 2010 Olympic Winter Games in Vancouver, British Columbia. With eight Olympic medals, Ohno is the most decorated US Winter Olympic athlete. He has also won 21 World Championship medals, eight of which are gold.

also contributed to a stereotype that Asian Americans are not athletic and prefer to be studying in school or in a science lab. In many cases, this stereotype may act as a barrier, limiting opportunities for talented Asian American athletes.

FINDING A PLACE TO PLAY

The players at the Bloomfield Dream League, an all-Asian basketball league in the Detroit area, have dealt with racial stereotypes their entire lives. "I play [basketball] pretty much every day and it's weird because when a lot of people are playing, no one wants to pick up an Asian kid," said Gonzalo Antonio, a Filipino American who is the captain of one of the teams in the Bloomfield Dream League. "They're thinking, well, 'Hey, he doesn't look the part, doesn't fit the mold, he probably can't play, can't hoop or anything.' You have to constantly prove yourself and it's kind of irritating."[5]

The athletes in the Bloomfield Dream League appreciate the opportunity that it gives them to play a game they love. In the past few years, the league has doubled in size. Tournaments with similar leagues in other cities have also helped Asian American athletes gain exposure nationally. "When you come here and you actually watch these guys who have played high school varsity, who have played in college, it's far from [the stereotypes]," said Ron Gayta, Bloomfield Dream League director. "We have guys who are

Natalie Chou puts up a shot for Baylor in a 2017 game.

just as athletic as anybody that's out there trying to make it big in any league. So, once you see it up live, in person, that stereotype is definitely squashed."[6]

Former Texas prep star Natalie Chou can relate. Chou played two years at Baylor University before transferring to the University of California, Los Angeles (UCLA) in 2018. She remembers the reactions she got from her opponents when her team entered a gym.

"I would walk past teams that we were about to play and I would hear, 'Oh! I got the Asian! That's me, I am guarding her!' Or, 'This is going to be the easiest game,'" said Chou. "And I would just start smiling because I was the best one on the team. . . . They think you are Asian and you can't really play sports. But usually in the first couple of seconds is when they realize, 'Oh snap!' I usually do a move and they are like, oh no, bad choice to guard me."[7]

"LINSANITY" BREAKING STEREOTYPES

In recent years, the success of Asian American athletes such as Jeremy Lin has helped break down stereotypes. In February 2012, "Linsanity" spread across the United States and throughout parts of Asia. As a relatively unknown second-year player, Jeremy Lin broke into the New York Knicks' starting lineup and had an immediate impact. Lin scored 28 points in a win against the Utah Jazz in his first career start. In his first five career starts, the 23-year-old player scored 136 points, more than legendary NBA stars such as Michael Jordan, Shaquille O'Neal, and Allen Iverson. His performance announced his arrival as one of the NBA's newest stars, an Asian American in a sport that featured few Asian players.

Jeremy Lin overcame numerous obstacles to carve out a long and prosperous NBA career.

Yet Lin's path to becoming an NBA star was not easy. In high school, he led his Palo Alto High School team to a state championship and was chosen as California's player of the year. Despite his athletic talent, his top choice, UCLA, did not offer him a basketball scholarship. Instead, Lin crossed the country to attend Harvard University, which did not offer athletic scholarships but did have a Division I basketball team. At Harvard, the 6-foot-3-inch (191 cm) point guard put up great numbers, averaging 15.5 points, 4.9 rebounds, 4.1 assists, and 2.3 steals per game over his final three seasons. In his junior and senior years, Lin was selected to the All–Ivy League First Team and was a finalist for the Bob Cousy Award for the nation's top point guard.

Despite these accomplishments, Lin was ignored in the 2010 NBA draft. He signed as a rookie free agent with the Golden State Warriors and worked in a development league to improve his strength and skills. After being waived by the Warriors and the Houston Rockets in 2011, Lin was picked up by the Knicks in December 2011. A few months later, he was a star.

Many people wonder how scouts and basketball insiders failed to identify Lin, a player who was barely recruited, undrafted, and cut by two NBA teams. Both Lin and former NBA commissioner David Stern believe that his Asian ethnicity had something to do with it. When asked why he didn't get a scholarship in college, Lin replied, "Well, the obvious thing in my mind is that I was Asian American which, you know, is a whole different issue but . . . I think that was a barrier."[8]

Stern agrees that stereotypes may have made it harder for Lin to break into professional basketball. "In terms of looking at somebody . . . I don't know whether he was discriminated against because he was at Harvard," he said. "Or because he was Asian."[9] Ultimately, Stern believes that Lin was at a disadvantage because he did not have the same background as the typical NBA player.

Lin's success on the court is helping to break down stereotypes about Asian American athletes. He has also become a role model for Asian Americans, showing that it is possible to succeed in professional sports regardless of a person's ethnic background.

PYEONGCHANG 2018

Asian American athletes also broke stereotypes at the 2018 Olympics in PyeongChang, South Korea. Bringing its most diverse group of athletes to the Winter Games, the US team spotlighted several Asian American

DEFYING ASIAN STEREOTYPES IN BASEBALL

In 2018, Shohei Ohtani made his major league baseball debut with the Los Angeles Angels and has been smashing balls and Asian stereotypes in baseball ever since. Many people expect Asian ball players to be small and fast athletes who put the ball into play and use their quickness to get on base. Ohtani, who is also a pitcher, is a power hitter known for driving the ball more than 400 feet. During one pregame batting practice in Denver, he hit several balls onto the stadium's third deck, one of which was estimated to have traveled an incredible 517 feet. Ohtani's power at the plate is proving that Asian baseball players can be big-time sluggers. Even more importantly, Ohtani is getting a lot of attention for simply being an exciting player to watch, regardless of his race.

INSPIRING THE NEXT GENERATION

Before Nathan Chen and the Shibutani siblings, there were Asian American skating stars Kristi Yamaguchi and Michelle Kwan. Together, these trailblazing athletes have inspired increasing numbers of Asian American athletes on the ice, while also encountering stereotypes on their rise to the highest levels of figure skating. At the 1992 Winter Olympics, Yamaguchi became the first Asian American woman to win a gold medal in figure skating. At the 1998 Winter Olympics, Kwan won the silver medal in ladies figure skating, while her teammate Tara Lipinski won the gold. After the event, MSNBC posted a headline online that read "American beats out Kwan" suggesting that Kwan was not an American citizen because of her Asian heritage. In February 2002, Kwan took the ice again at the Salt Lake City Winter Olympics and competed brilliantly. At home, 7 and 10 year old Alex and Maia Shibutani watched in awe. They wanted to be just like Kwan.[10]

athletes competing in a variety of sports, including snowboarding, figure skating, and speed skating. One of the superstars of the Games was 17-year-old Chloe Kim, a Korean American snowboarder. In the women's snowboard halfpipe event, Kim landed her signature back-to-back 1080s—three full revolutions on the same jump, a feat that no other female snowboarder has landed in competition— to win a gold medal. Even before the 2018 Olympics, Kim was a snowboarding star. At age 13, she qualified for the Sochi Games but could not compete because she was too young. At age 14, she won the first of four X Games titles. At 15, she scored a perfect 100 in competition, only the second halfpipe rider to do so. With her success on the halfpipe, Kim has become an inspiring role model for future generations of Asian American athletes.

Meanwhile, seven of the 14 members of the US figure skating team were Asian American. Many of these skaters starred on the Olympic stage. Japanese American Mirai Nagasu landed one of the most challenging jumps in figure skating, the triple axel, and helped Team USA win the bronze medal in the team competition. The brother and sister team of Maia and Alex Shibutani performed brilliantly in ice dance, winning a bronze medal and becoming the first Asian Americans to medal in ice dance. US national champion Nathan Chen landed an impressive six quadruple jumps in the men's long program. Together, these achievements highlighted the talent and strength of Asian American athletes, breaking stereotypes and providing inspiration to future generations of Asian American competitors.

DISCUSSION STARTERS

○ What stereotypes have you heard about Asian American athletes? What examples beyond those mentioned in this chapter disprove these stereotypes?

○ What athletic role models did you admire growing up? How did these athletes inspire you?

○ What effect do you think the Olympics has on sports stereotypes?

CHAPTER FIVE

WHITE SPORTS, BLACK SPORTS

R acial stereotypes suggest that white athletes are better at certain sports, such as swimming, tennis, golf, and hockey, while black athletes are better able to succeed at track, football, and basketball. However, history has shown that athletes of all races have excelled in every sport, even those traditionally considered "white" or "black" sports.

HOCKEY: A TRADITIONALLY WHITE SPORT

Ice hockey has long been a sport that features white players and fans in large numbers. As of 2015, only 5 percent of National Hockey League (NHL) players were black.[1] That's far less than the roughly 67 percent of NFL players and 80 percent of NBA players who identify as people of color. Growing up in California, writer Antonio De Loera-Brust was one of the only Latino players in his local hockey leagues. "When I played, other players of color were few and far between," he said. "One goalkeeper I played with was African American, and the daughter of Central American immigrants was one of the fiercest opponents I ever faced. Aside from a handful of Asian Americans, the rest of the kids were white."[2]

The lack of diversity in hockey extends from the ice to the fans. According to a 2013 Nielsen report, 92 percent of

Hockey can feel like an overwhelmingly white sport based not only on who plays the game but also on who watches it.

NHL viewers were white, while only 3 percent were black.[3] Other researchers studying the issue have found that the most significant factor driving fans to a sport is previous exposure and access to the sport. In other words, a person who grows up watching or playing hockey is more likely to be a hockey fan than someone who has not spent much time around the sport.

Experts believe that hockey's lack of diversity can be explained by a combination of factors. First, the sport has historically been most popular with people living in cold, northern countries such as Sweden, Russia, and Canada. In these colder climates, before the introduction of ice rinks, people could skate outside on canals and ponds for several months of the year. In southern countries, which have higher numbers of people of color, the climate is not suited to winter sports. As a result, people from these countries are less likely to have been exposed to winter sports like ice hockey and are less likely to have their children try an unfamiliar sport.

ECONOMIC BARRIERS

In addition to geographic barriers, the lack of diversity in ice hockey may also be explained by the high cost of the sport. In 2013, a study found that white American families have a median net worth 13 times greater than that of black families and ten times greater than that of Latino families.[4] That can be a problem for young athletes of color who want to play hockey. Unlike soccer or basketball, in which players need only a ball to kick or dribble, ice hockey requires expensive equipment—skates, pads, and sticks that can cost hundreds of dollars. In addition, the ice rinks where hockey practices and games occur—which are generally located in affluent neighborhoods and suburbs—are extremely expensive to maintain, and these costs are passed on to players and teams. "I was one of the rare Latinos who played hockey because my parents could afford to buy the gear," wrote De Loera-Brust.[6]

Economic barriers may also be a factor for the lack of diversity in several other traditionally "white" sports such as tennis and golf. The cost for equipment, greens fees, and country club memberships add up fast. Memberships in tennis clubs, lessons from coaches, and fees for tournaments can also be too expensive for the average family to afford, limiting the number of children exposed to the sport.

Sociologist Thomas C. Wilson has studied the connection between wealth and a person's likelihood of playing or attending a sport. "Those rich in economic capital

EFFORTS TO IMPROVE DIVERSITY

To make hockey more inclusive and diverse, the NHL and communities are working together to develop new programs that get inner-city kids playing hockey. In Chicago, the Blackhawks have a youth program called G. O. A. L. (Get Out and Learn) that introduces hockey to kids who might not otherwise have the chance to play it. The program brings hockey to schools, community centers, and other neighborhood places where kids can play in a structured environment. To help with the cost, the Blackhawks also donate full sets of hockey equipment to each school. In 2016, more than 90,000 kids at 160 Chicago-area schools participated in the program.[7] Retired NHL player Jamal Mayers is the Blackhawks Community Liaison and works with the G. O. A. L. program. He hopes that one day, a kid who goes through the G. O. A. L. program or a similar program in another city makes it to the NHL and becomes a role model for the next generation, proving that success in sports is colorblind.

are more involved in sports generally, presumably because they can better afford their cost, both in terms of money and leisure time," Wilson said.[8]

CULTURAL FACTORS

In addition to economic barriers, cultural factors may contribute to some sports being more segregated than others. Certain sports may attract people from a particular race not because they are biologically better at the sport, but because their culture values and embraces the sport. For example, Kenya is known for producing many world-class marathon runners because long distance running has been part of Kenyan culture for generations. In the same way, China produces many table tennis players because the game is a large part of Chinese culture. Because baseball is central to Latin American culture, Latin America produces many top baseball players.

In some cases, athletes may feel pressure from their communities to stick with the traditional sports valued by their culture. William Douglas started playing hockey at age 13 while growing up in Philadelphia. Today, he writes a blog about people of color in hockey. Douglas believes that hockey's lack of diversity comes in part from people of color shaming their peers for playing a sport that doesn't fit in with their cultural norms. "In our community, people still think [hockey] is a white sport. My black friends thought I was out of my mind," Douglas said.[9] "There's a perception in the African American community that we shouldn't like hockey or sports like NASCAR. Not seeing players of color on the ice on a regular basis or not knowing there are players of color that reinforces the stereotype. Then it became a self-fulfilling prophecy of sorts."[10]

CAN WHITE MEN JUMP?

While hockey has long been viewed as a stereotypical white sport, other stereotypes paint basketball as a black sport. With roughly 80 percent of NBA players coming from minority racial backgrounds, even NBA legend Larry Bird once said that basketball "is a black man's game, and it will be forever."[11]

Economic and cultural factors may attract more African American athletes to basketball. In comparison with sports like hockey or golf, basketball is inexpensive to play. The only equipment required is a ball and a pair of sneakers. Public courts

O'REE MAKES HISTORY

He was known as the Jackie Robinson of hockey. Willie O'Ree broke the color barrier in the NHL in 1958. That year he was playing in the Quebec Senior Hockey League when the Boston Bruins called him up to play two games. He played in 43 more games for the Bruins during the 1960–61 season and then returned to the minors for the rest of his career. Although his NHL career was short, O'Ree became an inspiration to hockey players of color who came after him.

TAUNTS AND STEREOTYPES

In February 2018, four fans were ejected from an NHL game in Chicago for making racially charged comments at Washington Capitals player Devante Smith-Pelly. As Smith-Pelly entered the penalty box in the game's third period, fans around the box began chanting "basketball, basketball, basketball" at him. When asked about the taunts, Smith-Pelly said it was pretty obvious that it was a racial stereotype that basketball is a "black" sport and hockey is for "white" athletes. After the incident, NHL commissioner Gary Bettman released a statement condemning the unacceptable behavior.

can be found in nearly every neighborhood, often with pickup games running at all hours of the day and night. In addition, basketball is an important part of African American culture. African American youth are more likely to pick up a basketball because they are encouraged to do so by adults and other community leaders and because basketball is seen as a way to express and empower themselves. In addition, there are a large number of black role models in basketball, which can influence youth to favor the sport.

Yet at the same time, white basketball players can also be successful on the court. Players such as Bird, Kevin Love, and Steve Nash have shown that talent, not race, makes a great basketball player. Chandler Parsons is a white forward for the NBA's Memphis Grizzlies. He says that it doesn't matter what race a person is, because once they step on the

Chandler Parsons is one of many white basketball players defying stereotypes in the NBA.

court, they are all just basketball players. "We play basketball because we play basketball," said Parsons. "We don't see color when we're playing basketball. It's about competing, camaraderie and having the ultimate goal of winning a championship. It doesn't matter if you're playing with a bunch of Europeans, black guys, Asian guys, Latin guys. It doesn't matter, because you guys are all there to do one thing, and that's playing basketball."[12]

Wayne Simmonds became a fan favorite for the Philadelphia Flyers.

BREAKING SPORTS STEREOTYPES

Sports stereotypes can be proven wrong, including those stemming from the comparisons of predominantly white and black sports. Athletes from all different backgrounds are showing the world that they can be successful regardless of their race or ethnicity. Black athletes such as swimmer Simone Manuel, gymnasts Simone Biles and Laurie Hernandez, golfer Tiger Woods, and tennis stars Serena and Venus Williams have risen to the pinnacle of traditionally "white" sports, proving that success comes in every color.

Even in hockey, diversity is improving and stereotypes are being broken. Players such as P. K. Subban, Wayne Simmonds, and Devante Smith-Pelly are showing game after game that non-white players can be successful in hockey. In 2018, Smith-Pelly played an important role in helping the Washington Capitals win their first Stanley Cup in team history. Smith-Pelly's path to the NHL was not easy. He bounced around seven different teams before just making the cut to become part of the Capitals. During the 2017–18 regular season, the 26-year-old player scored only a handful of goals. But he got hot in the playoffs, scoring seven goals as Washington stormed to the title.

During the Capitals' victory parade, fans chanted his initials and pumped their fists as he passed. For fans and young players, players like Smith-Pelly playing at hockey's highest level is helping to break stereotypes. "It also opens the door to let young black, African Americans know that, 'Hey I can do this,'" Capitals fan Alphonso Wilkins said. Caps fan Jody O'Keefe agreed, adding, "People of color can play hockey and not only get into the league but also thrive and play at a high level."[13]

DISCUSSION STARTERS

- What do you think sports leagues can do to attract more people from different races and backgrounds to play and watch a sport?
- Why do you think hockey has been slow to diversify—in terms of both its players and its fans?
- What other sports are linked to a particular race or ethnic group? Why does this happen?

CHAPTER SIX

STEREOTYPES AND SPORTS MASCOTS

Not all stereotypes in sports stem from activity on the field. Some stereotypes exist in the names and mascots chosen to represent teams. Across sport teams at many levels, from little leagues to professional leagues, numerous teams have branded themselves with names and mascots based on stereotypical depictions of Native Americans. Examples include MLB's Cleveland Indians and Atlanta Braves, the NFL's Washington Redskins, college football's Florida State Seminoles, and the NHL's Chicago Blackhawks.

A LONG HISTORY

Native American names have been used for decades in sports. For example, the Boston Braves adopted their team name in 1912. The Cleveland Indians were named in 1915. In the 1920s and 1930s, numerous high schools and colleges across the United States adopted similar team names. At the time, most Native Americans did not object to these team names. Experts say that many did not think of themselves as generalized "Indians" or "Braves."

"Indians didn't think of themselves as 'Indians' until well into the twentieth century," said Kevin Gover, director of the Smithsonian Institution's National Museum of the American Indian and a citizen of the Pawnee Tribe of Oklahoma.

Many Cleveland baseball fans openly embrace a mascot that is widely criticized for embodying racial stereotypes.

"They thought of themselves as members of their own individual tribes and nations. So a Lakota had as much in common with a Comanche as he did with a Frenchman, as far as they were concerned."[1]

However, as the years passed, many in the Native American community came to find the practice demeaning to their culture. They felt the sports names, mascots, and logos characterized their people in stereotypical fashion as vicious, savage warriors, rather than the three-dimensional people they are. In 1968, the National Congress of American Indians (NCAI) launched a campaign focusing on the stereotypes of Native Americans in pop culture and the media, including sports. As part of this effort, the NCAI called for the end of team names and mascots that perpetuate stereotypes of Native peoples.

HARMLESS OR HARMFUL?

For some people, the use of Native American names, images, and mascots is harmless. Supporters of these names and images argue that using them is a way to honor the history of Native Americans in the United States. In 2016, the *Washington Post* reported that 90 percent of Native Americans who responded to a poll said they were not offended by the Washington Redskins name. "I'm proud of being Native American and of the Redskins," said Barbara Bruce, a Chippewa teacher who has lived on a North Dakota reservation most of her life. "I'm not ashamed of that at all. I like that name."[2] Bruce and many other Native Americans who participated in the poll said they embrace the use of Native American imagery in sports because it brings attention to them in a society where they are not often represented. In fact, only 8 percent of those surveyed said that Native American imagery in sports bothered them.[3]

However, others disagree. Tara Houska is a tribal attorney and member of the Couchiching First Nation who lives in Washington, DC. She has organized protests against the Redskins name.

"A tomahawk chop and a bunch of people wearing redface does not honor me in any sense of the word, and it certainly does not honor Native American children," said Houska. She contends that the imagery used by the Redskins and other sports teams promotes damaging stereotypes of Native Americans. "Yes, it is offensive, and I

BATTLING NATIVE AMERICAN STEREOTYPES

Tristan Ahtone, an award-winning journalist and member of the Kiowa tribe of Oklahoma, is working to reduce stereotypes about Native Americans across all media, including sports. Ahtone was one of 24 journalists worldwide selected to attend Harvard University during the 2017–18 academic year to study as a Nieman Fellow. At Harvard, Ahtone is developing a set of guidelines for fair and accurate coverage of Native American lives and stories. It will help the media avoid using clichés, stereotypes, and racially insensitive terms when covering Native American stories and people. For example, Ahtone recommends identifying people by specific tribes, nations, or communities instead of saying they are part of a "Native American tribe." He also cautions the media to avoid using mythological creatures to explain complicated belief systems. Too often, the media approaches Native American stories by making them fit a stereotype. Yet Ahtone stresses that there is no typical Native American. Like all Americans, each Native American is unique.[4]

don't like seeing it everywhere. But what really matters is how this affects our youth," she said.[5]

Dr. Roger Dube, a Rochester Institute of Technology (RIT) professor and a Mohawk of the Turtle clan, also believes that images of Native Americans can be harmful. "The sports communities defend these images by saying, 'These are positive portrayals. We are showing Native Americans being strong, fierce and vicious, and those are the qualities we want our sports team to have,'" said Dube. "The problem is those images are destructive. It is not who we are and not who we were. It is not how we live. It tends to dehumanize the Native American communities by focusing on these caricatures."[6]

A movement to take action against the use of Native American nicknames is growing. In 2013, the Change the Mascot campaign was launched by activists aiming to convince the NFL to stop using the term "Redskins" as the name of the Washington football team. Campaign supporters argue that the term is used as a racial slur.

REINFORCING STEREOTYPES

In 2016, researchers from the University of Montana conducted a study to examine how being exposed to Native American sports mascots affected people. Some study participants viewed a Native American image, while others viewed an animal image. The researchers

Ray Halbritter, national representative of the Oneida Indian Nation, speaks at a Change the Mascot symposium in 2013.

then measured how strongly the participants associated Native Americans with being "warlike," a common Native American stereotype.

When asked directly, the participants reported no difference in how warlike they viewed Native Americans to be. However, when participants completed an indirect stereotype measure, those who had viewed the Native American image were more likely to associate warlike qualities with Native Americans. The study illustrates a concept called implicit bias, in which a subject has preconceived notions about others without realizing it. "Our participants were either unwilling to admit or unaware of the mascot's influence on their views of Native Americans," explained researcher Justin Angle. "Their bias was implicit, either hidden or incognizant."[7]

Angle cautions that implicit bias can have negative effects outside of sports. It can affect a variety of decisions, such as choosing who to hire or selecting who will be on a jury. And often, the people making biased decisions do not even realize they are doing it.

The researchers also studied whether attitudes toward Native Americans differed between people who lived in cities with Native American sports teams and those who did not. They found that people living in cities with Native American sports teams and mascots were more likely to view Native Americans as warlike. Then they took their research one step further and compared the attitudes in four cities: Cleveland and Atlanta, which have Native American mascots for their baseball teams, and Detroit and Miami, which have animals as team mascots. They found that Cleveland residents, whose mascot is considered to be one of the most offensive in sports, were more likely to associate Native Americans with warlike traits than people living in the other cities. "In other words, the more offensive the mascot, the greater the effect," wrote Angle.[8]

CHANGING NAMES AND MASCOTS

To avoid promoting stereotypes of Native Americans, some leagues and teams have chosen to change their team names and mascots. In 2012, the state of Oregon announced that all public schools would discontinue use of Native American names and mascots such as "Indians," "Chiefs," "Braves," and "Redskins." In college athletics, scores of schools have changed team names to remove Native American references. For example, Stanford University changed its team name from "Indians" to "Cardinal." The Saint John's University Redmen became the Red Storm in 1994. The University of North Dakota changed from the Fighting Sioux to the Fighting Hawks. Other schools, such as Illinois, kept their team name—the Fighting Illini—but dropped "Chief Illiniwek" as its official mascot.

In pro sports, some teams that have retained their Indian names have altered or changed their mascots. In 1986, the Atlanta Braves

ONGOING DEBATE

In 2018, a Cincinnati-area high school debated whether to keep its team nickname and mascot, the Redskins. After two and a half hours of discussion, a committee decided to allow Anderson High School to keep its more than 80-year-old name and mascot. Supporters of the name argued that it was part of the school's tradition and changing it would cost the school hundreds of thousands of dollars. Those opposed to the name argued that it was offensive and racist. Committee members said that they had been bullied and received threats from people on both sides of the issue.

University of Illinois mascot Chief Illiniwek is one of many that have been retired after complaints that they perpetuate negative racial stereotypes.

retired their mascot, Chief Noc-A-Homa. The Chief had a tepee in the left-field stands, and when a Braves player hit a home run, the Chief would come out and perform a celebration dance.

In 2018, the Cleveland Indians announced that they would no longer use their Chief Wahoo logo on their uniforms or on banners and signs in the stadium, beginning in 2019. Chief Wahoo is a cartoon character that first appeared on the Indians' uniforms in 1948. After years of protests, the Indians organization finally agreed to remove the image. "We have consistently maintained that we are cognizant and sensitive to both sides of the discussion," said Indians' chairman and chief executive Paul Dolan in a statement issued by MLB. "While we recognize many of our fans have a longstanding attachment to Chief Wahoo, I'm ultimately in agreement with Commissioner Manfred's desire to remove the logo from our uniforms in 2019."[9]

LEGAL CHALLENGES

While some teams have voluntarily changed names and mascots, others have resisted. Washington Redskins owner Daniel Snyder has repeatedly refused to change his team's name. In a letter to fans in 2013, Snyder defended his decision. "I respect the feelings of those who are offended by the team name. But I hope such individuals also try to respect what the name means, not only for all of us in the extended Washington Redskins family, but among Native Americans too," he said. "After 81 years, the team name 'Redskins' continues to hold the memories and meaning of where we came from, who we are, and who we want to be in the years to come," Snyder added.[10]

Yet others disagree. The Oneida Indian Nation launched a national "Change the Mascot" public relations campaign, aimed at putting pressure on the Redskins and other sports teams to get rid of Native American names and mascots. Even former president Barack Obama said in 2013 that he'd think about changing the Redskins name if he were the team's owner.

In 1992, seven Native American activists legally challenged the Redskins and filed a petition with the US Patent and Trademark Office. The petition asked for the team's trademark registration to be revoked. The patent and trademark office's appeals board ruled for the activists, but the team continued to fight and argued that the majority of Native Americans were not offended by the Redskins

SEMINOLE APPROVAL

In some cases, Native American tribes have approved the use of their names by sports teams. The Seminole Tribe of Florida has approved Florida State University's Seminole nickname. The tribe even helped university representatives create a costume for the team's mascot, Chief Osceola, giving approval for his face paint, flaming spear, and Appaloosa horse.

name and the activists did not prove that the name was used as a slur. For nearly 25 years, the two sides battled in the courts. Then, in 2017, the Supreme Court issued a ruling that a federal law banning trademarks that "may disparage" people was a violation of the US Constitution's First Amendment, which guarantees the freedom of speech. Because the Native American activists had relied on this section of law for their case against the Redskins, they now had little legal standing to argue the Redskins should lose their trademark registration.

Jesse Witten, an attorney representing the Native Americans, says that even though they lost the legal case, the publicity it generated was positive. "There's the legal case and then there's the cause," he said. "It was a galvanizing force that caused people to pay attention to the cause."[11]

DISCUSSION STARTERS

o   Do you think using an ethnic group or race as a team name or mascot is harmless or harmful? Explain your position.

o   How do you think using Native American team names and mascots could contribute to stereotypes?

o   Some sports teams use names that depict other cultures, such as the Notre Dame Fighting Irish. Do you think these types of names contribute to stereotypes? Explain.

CHAPTER SEVEN

SPORTS MEDIA AND RACIAL STEREOTYPES

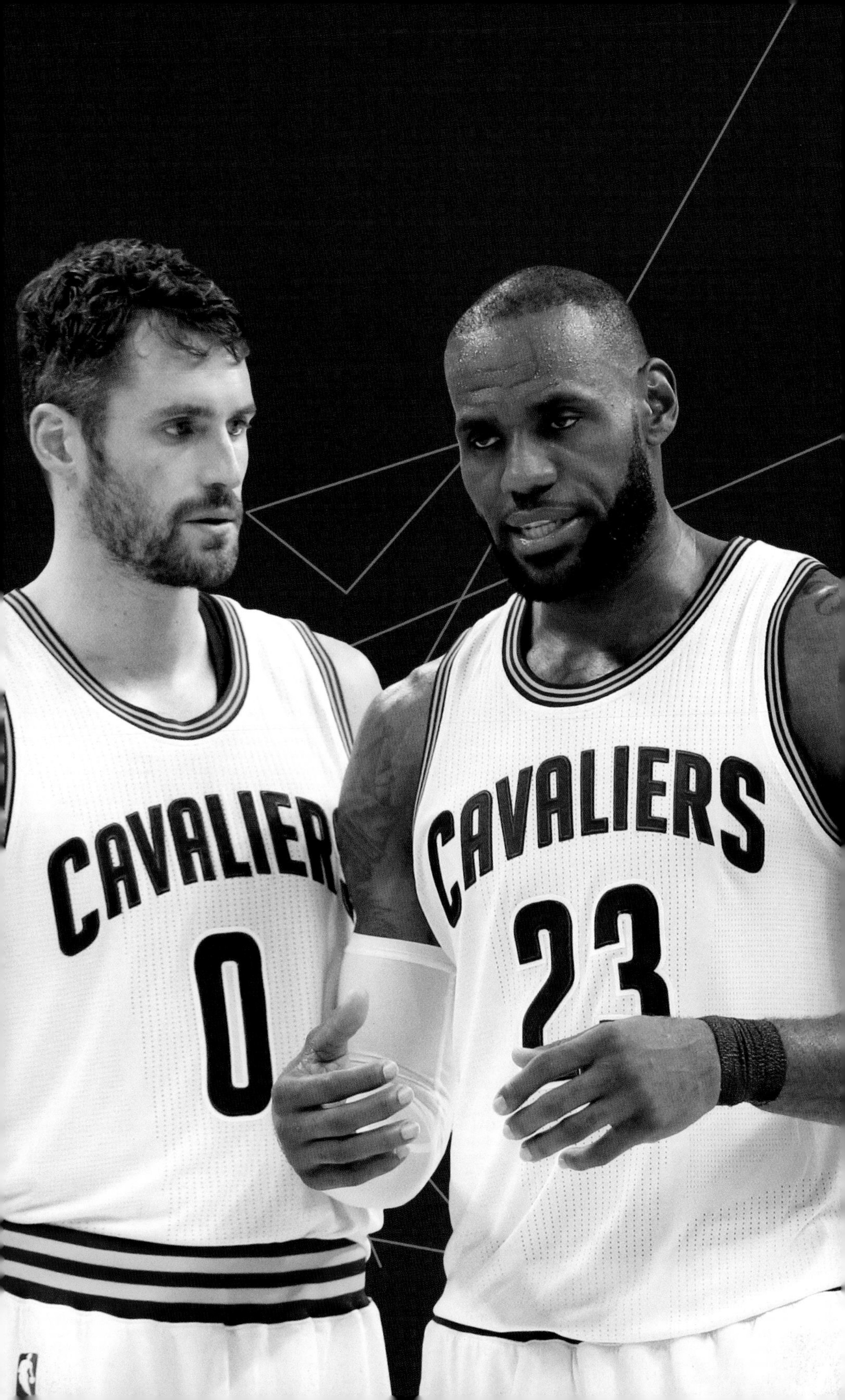
CAVALIERS
0
CAVALIERS
23

The way the media presents athletes can contribute to race-based stereotypes in sports. Both the language used to talk about athletes of different races and the stories the media chooses to feature can shape the way the public sees race, athletes, and sport.

The words and phrases that journalists choose to describe and talk about athletes can carry implicit racial bias. Implicit bias refers to the attitudes or stereotypes that unconsciously affect how a person thinks and behaves. Implicit biases can be positive or negative. They are often unconscious and are activated without a person even being aware of them. An implicit association causes a person to feel a certain way about another person based on race, ethnicity, age, or appearance. These associations develop over a person's lifetime, beginning at a very young age. In addition to personal experiences, the media is often a source of implicit associations.

Several studies have looked at how race is approached in sports journalism. The large majority of this research suggests that white athletes are described much differently by journalists than their non-white teammates. Some of the earliest research, by Raymond Rainville and Edward McCormick, looked at NFL broadcasts in 1977. They found

The choice of which stories you get to read in a newspaper can be subject to bias.

that black players were more likely to be criticized when a bad play occurred, while white players were more likely to be praised for good plays.[1]

In 1996, another study by James Rada of Ithaca College looked at NFL broadcast comments. The study found that when journalists described white players, they highlighted intelligence, but they focused on physical qualities when describing black players. In a 2005 follow-up study, Rada examined sports journalism in college football and basketball games. Although he found that positive comments about an athlete's intelligence were made equally about white and black players, negative comments

In addition to racial stereotypes, athletes also face gender stereotypes in the media. Comments like "girl push-ups" and "throwing like a girl" put down girls and imply that they are inferior athletes. In 2016, a study by Cambridge University Press found that the media talks about male athletes two to three times more than female athletes. Key words that were more likely to appear in discussions of male athletes included *fast*, *strong*, *beat*, *win*, and *dominate*. Female athletes were more likely to be associated with terms such as *aged*, *pregnant*, *married*, *compete*, *participate*, and *strive*. This language shows the bias associating women with appearance and family status and implying they have less athletic ability.[3]

about intelligence were more often directed toward black players. In addition, white players received more positive comments about their character, while black players were more likely to be described with negative character comments.[2]

The use of stereotyping language extends to sports beyond football. In a 2001 study, researchers from Clemson University and Indiana University examined the language used by college basketball announcers. Their study showed that stereotypes were embedded throughout game broadcasts. The announcers' comments reinforced stereotypical ideas related to the superior athletic ability of black players and the leadership and intelligence of white players, ideas that can have unfortunate repercussions throughout society. "The words of sportscasters—repeated hundreds, even thousands, of times by different announcers in similar ways—provide a conceptual frame for the sports experience, and that mental frame has particular importance because fans often apply it to nonathletic situations," the researchers wrote.[4]

STORIES CHOSEN BY THE MEDIA

Research shows that the media can affect people's thoughts and actions. Beyond the language used in the media, the types of stories about athletes that the sports media chooses to run can shape the way people view athletes and sports. To explore how the media influences the public's view of athletes, Cynthia Frisby, an associate professor of strategic communication at the University of Missouri, studied how the media presents stories about athletes. In her study, Frisby reviewed 155 news articles about male athletes. She gathered the articles from both online and print news sources. For each article, Frisby identified an overall theme, which included crime, domestic violence, training and hard work, moral successes and failures, violating sporting league rules, accomplishments, and personal lifestyles.

In 2015, Frisby presented her findings. Overall, she found that the media wrote slightly more stories about white athletes (43 percent) than black athletes (39 percent). However, she found that the stories about black athletes were significantly more negative. Stories about crime involved black athletes 66 percent of the time, as compared with 22 percent involving whites. Domestic violence stories featured black athletes 70 percent of the time, compared with only 17 percent for white athletes. In addition, 53 percent of stories about black athletes had an overall negative tone, as compared with only 27 percent of stories about white athletes.[5]

Frisby believes that more research is needed in the future to examine how the media covers athletes from different ethnic backgrounds, and that journalists and reporters should examine how their own biases contribute to the negative stereotyping of black athletes. "Not only does negative media coverage serve to legitimize social power inequalities, but also it is likely to undermine black athletes' achievements and contribute to stereotype threat," she said.[6]

Many experts were not surprised by Frisby's findings and say that they reflect a broader problem of how the media

BIAS BY OMISSION

Sometimes bias in sports media occurs when a report leaves out one side of the story. Bias by omission presents facts that support only a particular point of view or belief. Bias by omission can occur in a single story. It can also happen over time when a news outlet repeatedly reports only one side of events. For example, when a news story presents only certain facts about an athlete that fit a stereotype while omitting other details that don't fit the stereotype, it is an example of bias by omission.

covers African Americans and people of color in general. Dr. Robert A. Bennett III, instructor in African American studies at Ohio State University, noted that black people protesting the death of Freddie Gray, a Baltimore man who died in police custody, were vilified and called "thugs" by the media. He compared the coverage with that of a shootout between white biker gangs in 2015 that left nine people dead in Waco, Texas, in which "no such terminology was ever used, and it was reported these guys had hundreds of weapons stashed. It should not be surprising

STEREOTYPING COACHES

Language with a racial bias can also be found in stories written about coaches and other sports professionals. A 2010 study at Texas A&M University examined news releases announcing the hiring of NCAA football coaches. Such releases are typically written by college sports information directors (SIDs). The study found that in media reports about these hirings, white coaches were more frequently praised for their coaching abilities and experience, while black coaches were more likely to be discussed as being good recruiters and being able to monitor athletes (most of whom are African Americans) on the team. "The results also support [the] notion that the media help craft and shape our worldviews while also demonstrating who has power and who does not," wrote the researchers.[7]

The study suggested that training and education for SIDs could promote more inclusive language choices in the media, who base their stories on the releases provided by the SIDs. Although it would be just one small step toward breaking down sports stereotypes, the study's authors explain, "Collectively, little changes—such as press releases that do not perpetuate the dominant racial ideology—can amount to meaningful transformation."[8]

Venus, left, and Serena Williams have each won multiple Olympic gold medals.

because historically it has been natural practice to paint the activities of Black people in a negative light."[9]

UNEQUAL COVERAGE IN RIO

The media coverage of the 2016 Summer Olympics in Rio de Janeiro provided several examples of unequal treatment of athletes of different races. One of the most glaring occurred after Simone Manuel's historic race to win a gold medal in swimming's 100-meter freestyle race. The San Jose *Mercury News* reported Manuel's win with the headline "Phelps

Shares Historic Night with African American." The headline highlighted how the media spotlights the achievements of white male athletes—in this case Michael Phelps—and brushes over the accomplishments of non-white athletes. Later, the newspaper apologized for its biased coverage and updated the headline to include Manuel's name.

In another example, BBC broadcaster John Inverdale congratulated England's Andy Murray for being the first person to win two Olympic gold medals in tennis. However, Murray corrected him. The American sisters Venus and Serena Williams have each won four gold medals—one each in singles and three in doubles.

The media is a powerful influence that can shape how people see the world around them. Being aware of the ways bias and stereotyping can exist in the media is the first step toward eliminating them.

DISCUSSION STARTERS

- Read through the sports page of your local newspaper or online news source. What examples can you find of words that support stereotypes? How could you present the information differently so as to not use stereotypes?

- What examples of sports stereotypes have you noticed in movies and television?

- Do you think hiring more people of color in sports newsrooms will help reduce stereotypes in sports media?

CHAPTER EIGHT

THE EFFECT OF STEREOTYPES IN SPORTS

Stereotypes can have many effects, both on and off the field. There is growing evidence that stereotypes, even positive ones, can lead to generalized beliefs that spill into everyday life. They can unfairly and sometimes even unintentionally affect how a person thinks and behaves toward others. The good news, however, is that it is possible to overcome stereotypes.

STEREOTYPE THREAT

A growing number of studies suggests that stereotypes can directly impact how an athlete performs on the field. This phenomenon is known as stereotype threat. When athletes are reminded of a negative stereotype that includes them— such as black people can't swim or Asians are not athletic— part of their attention focuses on the fear of proving the stereotype true. Whether conscious or unconscious, this increased worry can interfere with the automatic responses that the athlete has fine-tuned in training. These responses are necessary to perform at the highest levels during a game or competition. "We have practiced these actions a lot, we perform them without monitoring them," said Sarah Martiny, an associate social psychology professor at the Arctic University of Norway. "What negative stereotypes can do is accentuate a worry component."[1] As a result, athletes overthink their movements, which can bring down their performance.

The effect of stereotype threat is often small—a single point or a few fractions of a second. Other factors, such as training and practice, have a much larger impact on an athlete's performance. However, for elite athletes, the difference between winning and losing is often extremely small. For example, Simone Manuel's gold-winning time in the 100-meter freestyle swim at the 2016 Summer Olympics was 52.70 seconds. The third-place finisher's time was 52.99, only 0.29 seconds behind. As a result, even the tiniest hesitation can have a significant effect on an athlete's performance.

Martiny says that one way athletes can counter stereotype threat is to replace the negative association with a positive one. In one study, Martiny and other scientists tested the effect of stereotype threat on female

DOWNSIDE OF A POSITIVE STEREOTYPE

So what's wrong with a positive stereotype, such as one that says African Americans are good at basketball or that Asians are smart? A stereotype is a generalization. When people do not live up to positive stereotypes, they can feel like failures. And those who do live up to them might not get credit for their hard work. For example, when an African American teen makes his high school varsity basketball team, people might think he's just naturally athletic and not see the hours and hours of practice he put in before the tryouts.

soccer and basketball players. Athletes who were reminded of their gender before a game performed worse than expected. Those who were reminded that they were part of a well-trained team typically outperformed their usual standards. Martiny says that coaches can help athletes by making positive associations in their pregame and sideline pep talks, such as reminding the athletes about how prepared they are. Strong role models can also reduce the effect of stereotype threat, giving athletes real-life examples of people who have succeeded in a sport.[2]

EFFECTS OFF THE FIELD

Stereotypes in sports can also affect people off the field. They influence how people think about others. While some people might align with aspects of a stereotype—for example, an Asian person who is not a good athlete—the problem with stereotypes is that they generalize about an entire group of people. This overgeneralization can blind people to the actual characteristics of people in that group and those in other groups. For example, using the stereotype that Asians are not athletic, a person is more likely to notice Asians who stumble on the track or miss a basketball shot. Noticing these things reinforces the stereotype that Asians are not athletic. If a person sees an Asian athlete scoring a basket or swimming fast, they might explain it as a lucky accident or the exception to the norm.

With many events being decided by fractions of seconds or points, even the slightest disadvantage from stereotype threat can be costly.

Or they might attribute the athlete's success to the individual performer instead of crediting it to the athlete's race. In addition, a person is also less likely to notice athletes of other races not performing well.

"This is especially true if the group to which we tie those people has an opposite stereotype applied to them," wrote Sally Raskoff, a sociology professor at Los Angeles Valley College. "This process is insidious and subconscious. We often act on it without thinking."[3]

For athletes, stereotypes on the field can have a real impact off the field. For example, when a black athlete is labeled with the stereotype of being a natural athletic talent with superior physical skills, it gives the athlete no advantage when interviewing for a job in the real world.

In comparison, white athletes may find that stereotypes of them being hardworking, intelligent, and disciplined help them land a job because employers want to hire people with these characteristics. In addition, sports stereotypes—whether positive or negative—are generalizations that are the beginnings of racism and race-based discrimination.

OVERCOMING SPORTS STEREOTYPES

Most people agree that overcoming stereotypes and seeing people as individuals benefits all. One of the first steps to overcoming stereotypes is to admit that they exist and are impossible to avoid, given how deeply embedded they are in American culture. Terri Adams-Fuller, an associate professor at Howard University, said, "The lessons we were taught as children about different racial/ethnic groups, gender differences, and sexual orientation shape our perceptions of others. These symbols are displayed in various forms, including the use of images, and the use of language describing 'good' and 'bad' in this society."[6] Many of these biases are implicit—conscious or unconscious thinking that can influence behavior and decisions.

Awareness is one way to overcome stereotypes. When a spotlight shines awareness on stereotypes and bias, it can help overcome them. For example, in a study of racial bias among NBA referees, a group of researchers found that referee calls were influenced by racial bias. However, after the study was made public and received widespread attention, a follow-up study found no racial bias in the referees' calls. The second study's results suggest that calling attention to bias can help reduce its effect on decision making.

Stereotypes can also be broken by seeking out examples of people who don't fit a particular stereotype. In sports, when more exposure is given to athletes like gymnast Simone Biles and basketball star Jeremy Lin who don't fit into sports stereotypes, the weaker these stereotypes will become. In addition, seeking specific characteristics about individual athletes—rather than lumping them into a generalized stereotype about their racial or ethnic group— can help people view athletes as they truly are.

One of the most effective ways to overcome stereotypes, both in sports and in the real world, is to make an effort to develop positive relationships with people of another race or ethnic group. Exposing children to people of different races at a young age can help reduce racial stereotypes and bias. Researchers believe that getting children involved in sports early in life is one way to break down racial bias and promote inclusiveness. Through youth sports, children can meet and play with diverse teammates and coaches. They learn the value of cooperation and teamwork with people of all races. They also develop personal relationships with children of other races, which help them see people as individuals instead of just representatives of a stereotype.

"Mere contact between group members isn't enough; what's important is meaningful, ongoing relations," wrote Linda Tropp, a psychology professor at the University of Massachusetts Amherst, and Rachel Godsil, a law professor at Seton Hall University School of Law.[7] Participating in situations in which members of different racial and ethnic groups can interact meaningfully and equally—such as on a sports team—is a particularly good way to break down stereotypes and implicit bias.

"If we want to get closer to the American ideal of equality, we must be open to identifying our individual biases, and becoming aware of how they impact our

Playing on a sports team together is one of the best ways to help kids interact with people from different backgrounds.

interactions and decisions," wrote Adams-Fuller. "It is only then that we can reach what Martin Luther King Jr. so eloquently stated about his dreams for his descendants—that they 'will one day live in a nation where they will not be judged by the color of their skin but by the content of their character.'"[8]

DISCUSSION STARTERS

- Do you think players in certain sports are more likely to face stereotype threat? Why or why not?
- How would you feel if somebody assumed they knew how you would perform a task based on your physical attributes?
- Do you think athletes of color always perform better when playing for a coach of the same race? Why or why not?

ESSENTIAL FACTS

SIGNIFICANT EVENTS

- In 1946, Jackie Robinson breaks the color line in major league baseball, becoming the first African American to play in the league.

- In 1988, Washington Redskins quarterback Doug Williams leads his team to victory in the Super Bowl, proving that a black quarterback can win in football's biggest game.

- In 2016, Simone Manuel becomes the first African American woman to win an individual Olympic gold medal in swimming at the Rio Olympic Games.

- In 2018, black Canadian Devante Smith-Pelly is a key part of the Washington Capitals playoff run to win hockey's Stanley Cup.

- In 2018, the Cleveland Indians announce that they will remove the controversial Chief Wahoo logo from their uniforms and stadium banners and signs.

KEY PLAYERS

- Cynthia Frisby, an associate professor of strategic communication at the University of Missouri, conducted research that shows how the sports media perpetuates race-based stereotypes.

- Daniel Snyder, owner of the NFL's Washington Redskins, refused to change his team name despite intense public pressure and has prevailed in a lawsuit aimed at forcing him to change the name.

IMPACT ON SOCIETY

Throughout sports, stereotypes are common. They affect athletes of different races in a wide variety of sports. Some stereotypes focus on an athlete's race, while others involve gender. Problems arise when people believe that stereotypes are true in all cases and use them to put expectations and limitations on athletes. For example, a college coach may not offer a scholarship to a talented Asian American basketball player simply because the coach is influenced, knowingly or unknowingly, by the stereotype that Asians are not good athletes. In this way, stereotypes and bias can unfairly and sometimes unintentionally take opportunities away from talented athletes of different racial and ethnic backgrounds.

QUOTE

"I would like there to be a day where there are more of us, and it's not 'Simone, the black swimmer.' The title 'black swimmer' makes it seem like I'm not supposed to be able to win a gold medal, or I'm not supposed to be able to break records. And that's not true."

—Simone Manuel

GLOSSARY

activist

A person who campaigns to bring about political or social change.

bias

Prejudice in favor of or against one thing, person, or group compared with another, usually in a way considered to be unfair.

campaign

A planned series of activities designed to produce a particular result, such as a political or social goal.

community

A group of people living together in the same place or having a particular characteristic in common.

discrimination

Unfair treatment of other people, usually because of race, age, or gender.

diversity

The inclusion of different types of people (of different races, genders, sexual orientations, disability statuses, and cultures) in an organization.

economic barriers

The costs incurred to join a new activity.

ethnicity

Belonging to a group that has a common national or cultural tradition.

generalization

A broad statement or an idea that is applied to a group of people or things.

implicit bias

Attitudes or stereotypes that unconsciously affect how a person thinks and behaves.

inclusive

Accepting of all people.

insidious

Proceeding in a gradual, subtle way, but with harmful effects.

omission

Something that is left out and not included.

segregated

Separated based on race, gender, ethnicity, or other factors.

stereotype

A widely held but oversimplified idea about a particular type of

ADDITIONAL RESOURCES

SELECTED BIBLIOGRAPHY

Arnett, Autumn. "Media Fuels Negative Perception of Black Athletes." *Diverse Issues in Higher Education*, 4 June 2015. diverseeducation.com. Accessed 17 Aug. 2018.

Judd, Wes. "Why the Ice Is White." *Pacific Standard Magazine*, 19 June 2015. psmag.com. Accessed 17 Aug. 2018.

Powell, Michael. "Warren Moon, Who Helped Clear Way for Black Quarterbacks, Recalls His Struggles." *New York Times*, 5 Feb. 2016. nytimes.com. Accessed 17 Aug. 2018.

FURTHER READINGS

Frisby, Cynthia M. *How You See Me, How You Don't*. Tate Publishing, 2015.

McClure, Stephanie M., and Cherise A. Harris, eds. *Getting Real about Race*. SAGE, 2018.

Proudfit, Joely. *Beyond the American Indian Stereotype: There's More to Me Than What You See (Intersections of Race, Ethnicity, and Culture)*. Praeger, 2019.

ONLINE RESOURCES

Booklinks
NONFICTION NETWORK
FREE! ONLINE NONFICTION RESOURCES

SOURCE NOTES

CHAPTER 1. A HISTORIC FIRST

1. Jesse Washington. "A New Chapter for Black Olympic Swimming." *Undefeated*, 12 Aug. 2016. theundefeated.com. Accessed 19 Sept. 2018.

2. Washington, "A New Chapter for Black Olympic Swimming."

3. Washington, "A New Chapter for Black Olympic Swimming."

4. Katie Rogers. "A Closer Look at Simone Manuel, Olympic Medalist, History Maker." *New York Times*, 13 Aug. 2016. nytimes.com. Accessed 19 Sept. 2018.

5. Washington, "A New Chapter for Black Olympic Swimming."

6. Washington, "A New Chapter for Black Olympic Swimming."

CHAPTER 2. HISTORY OF RACE AND SPORTS

1. "Negro Leagues History." *Negro Leagues Baseball Museum*. n.d. nlbm.com. Accessed 19 Sept. 2018.

2. Richard Lapchick. "The 2017 Racial and Gender Report Card: College Sport." *Institute for Diversity and Ethics in Sport*, 28 Feb. 2018. tidesport.org. Accessed 19 Sept. 2018.

3. Lapchick, "The 2017 Racial and Gender Report Card: College Sport."

CHAPTER 3. ATHLETIC OR INTELLIGENT?

1. William Weinbaum. "The Legacy of Al Campanis." *ESPN*, 1 Apr. 2012. espn.com. Accessed 19 Sept. 2018.

2. Weinbaum, "The Legacy of Al Campanis."

3. Maria Wilhelm. "In America's National Pastime, Says Frank Robinson, White Is the Color of the Game Off the Field." *People*, 27 Apr. 1987. people.com. Accessed 19 Sept. 2018.

4. Jonathan Abrams. "Auriemma Says Perceptions of Stanford Based on Race." *New York Times*, 4 Apr. 2009. nytimes.com. Accessed 19 Sept. 2018.

5. Michael Powell. "Warren Moon, Who Helped Clear Way for Black Quarterbacks, Recalls His Struggles." *New York Times*, 5 Feb. 2016. nytimes.com. Accessed 19 Sept. 2018.

6. Powell, "Warren Moon, Who Helped Clear Way for Black Quarterbacks, Recalls His Struggles."

7. Powell, "Warren Moon, Who Helped Clear Way for Black Quarterbacks, Recalls His Struggles."

8. Liz Clarke. "Doug Williams's Super Bowl Win 30 Years Ago Changed the Game for Black Quarterbacks." *Washington Post*, 30 Jan. 2018. washingtonpost.com. Accessed 19 Sept. 2018.

9. Clifton B. Parker. "Stereotypes Can Affect Athletes' Academic Performance, Stanford Researcher Says." *Stanford Report*, 26 Mar. 2014. news.stanford.edu. Accessed 19 Sept. 2018.

10. Trent Knoss. "Racial Stereotypes Influence Perception of NFL Quarterbacks." *CU Boulder Today*, 21 Aug. 2017. colorado.edu/today. Accessed 19 Sept. 2018.

11. Alejandro Danois. "The Black QB Stereotype Doug Williams Crushed 30 Years Ago Continues." *Shadow League*, 25 Jan. 2018. theshadowleague.com. Accessed 19 Sept. 2018.

CHAPTER 4. TOO SMALL, TOO SLOW?

1. Dave Roos. "Why Aren't There More Asian Americans in Pro Team Sports?" *HowStuffWorks*, 9 May 2017. howstuffworks.com. Accessed 19 Sept. 2018.

2. Jamilah King. "The Asian American Basketball Leagues That Helped Create Linsanity." *Colorlines*, 21 Feb. 2012. colorlines.com. Accessed 19 Sept. 2018.

3. Roos, "Why Aren't There More Asian Americans in Pro Team Sports?"

4. Roos, "Why Aren't There More Asian Americans in Pro Team Sports?"

5. Charlie Lapastora. "Local Leagues Open Opportunities for Asian Americans on the Basketball Court." *NBC News*, 27 Oct. 2015. nbcnews.com. Accessed 19 Sept. 2018.

6. Lapastora, "Local Leagues Open Opportunities for Asian Americans on the Basketball Court."

7. Ohm Youngmisuk. "Why Jeremy Lin and Jason Terry Are Rooting for Natalie Chou." *ESPN*, 3 Dec. 2016. espn.com. Accessed 19 Sept. 2018.

8. "Houston Rockets' Jeremy Lin on Asian Stereotypes." *CBS News*, 5 Apr. 2013. cbsnews.com. Accessed 19 Sept. 2018.

9. "Houston Rockets' Jeremy Lin on Asian Stereotypes."

10. Audrey Cleo Yap. "Stars of U.S. Figure Skating Team Find Strength in Past Olympians." *NBC News*, 10 Feb. 2018. nbcnews.com. Accessed 19 Sept. 2018.

CHAPTER 6. STEREOTYPES AND SPORTS MASCOTS

1. Erik Brady. "The Real History of Native American Team Names." *USA Today*, 24 Aug. 2016. usatoday.com. Accessed 19 Sept. 2018.

2. John Woodrow Cox, Scott Clement, and Theresa Vargas. "New Poll Finds 9 in 10 Native Americans Aren't Offended by Redskins Name." *Washington Post*, 19 May 2016. washingtonpost.com. Accessed 19 Sept. 2018.

3. Cox, Clement, and Vargas, "New Poll Finds 9 in 10 Native Americans Aren't Offended by Redskins Name."

4. Liz Mineo. "Battling Stereotypes of Native Americans." *Harvard Gazette*. 20 Mar. 2018. news.harvard.edu. Accessed 19 Sept. 2018.

5. Cox, Clement, and Vargas, "New Poll Finds 9 in 10 Native Americans Aren't Offended by Redskins Name."

6. Christopher Barilla. "Native American Mascots in Pro Sports." *Reporter*, 19 Feb. 2018. reporter. rit.edu. Accessed 19 Sept. 2018.

7. Justin Angle. "New Research Shows How Native American Mascots Reinforce Stereotypes." *Conversation*, 12 Sep 2016. theconversation.com. Accessed 19 Sept. 2018.

8. Angle, "New Research Shows How Native American Mascots Reinforce Stereotypes."

9. David Waldstein. "Cleveland Indians Will Abandon Chief Wahoo Logo Next Year." *New York Times*, 29 Jan. 2018. nytimes.com. Accessed 19 Sept. 2018.

10. Alison Harding. "Washington Redskins Team Owner Dan Snyder Defends Team Name in Letter." *CNN*, 10 Oct. 2013. cnn.com. Accessed 19 Sept. 2018.

11. Ian Shapira and Ann E. Marimow. "Washington Redskins Win Trademark Fight over the Team's Name." *Washington Post*, 29 June 2017. washingtonpost.com. Accessed 19 Sept. 2018.

CHAPTER 7. SPORTS MEDIA AND RACIAL STEREOTYPES

1. John Carvalho. "Sports Media Is Still Racist against Black Athletes." *Vice Sports*. 3 Oct. 2014. sports.vice.com. Accessed 19 Sept. 2018.

2. Carvalho, "Sports Media Is Still Racist against Black Athletes."

3. Carrie Oillaux. "How Language Shapes Gender Stereotypes in Sport." *sportanddev.org*. 23 May 2017. sportanddev.org. Accessed 19 Sept. 2018.

4. Andrew Billings and Susan Tyler Eastman. "Biased Voices of Sports: Racial and Gender Stereotyping in College Basketball Announcing." *Howard Journal of Communication*, vol. 10, 2010. 183–201. Accessed 19 Sept. 2018.

5. Nathan Hurst. "Black Athletes Stereotyped Negatively in Media Compared to White Athletes." *University of Missouri School of Journalism*, 2 June 2015. journalism.missouri.edu. Accessed 19 Sept. 2018.

6. Hurst, "Black Athletes Stereotyped Negatively in Media Compared to White Athletes."

7. George Cunningham and Trevor Bopp. "Race Ideology Perpetuated: Media Representations of Newly Hired Football Coaches." *Journal of Sports Media*, vol. 5, no 1, Spring 2010. 1–19. Accessed 19 Sept. 2018.

8. Cunningham and Bopp, "Race Ideology Perpetuated: Media Representations of Newly Hired Football Coaches."

9. Arnett, Autumn. "Media Fuels Negative Perception of Black Athletes," *Diverse: Issues in Higher Education*, 4 June 2015. diverseeducation.com. Accessed 19 Sept. 2018.

CHAPTER 8. THE EFFECT OF STEREOTYPES IN SPORTS

1. Alexandra Ossola. "How Stereotypes Slow Athletes Down." *Nautilus*, 24 Aug. 2016. nautil.us. Accessed 19 Sept. 2018.

2. Ossola, "How Stereotypes Slow Athletes Down."

3. Sally Raskoff. "The Impact of Stereotyping." *Everyday Sociology*, 11 June 2012. everydaysociologyblog.com. Accessed 19 Sept. 2018.

4. Richard Lapchick. "The 2017 Racial and Gender Report Card: National Football League." *Institute for Diversity and Ethics in Sport*, 18 Feb. 2017. tidesport.org. Accessed 19 Sept. 2018.

5. Mina Kimes. "New Study Exposes the NFL's Real Coaching Diversity Crisis." *ESPN*, 12 Jan. 2016. espn.com. Accessed 19 Sept. 2018.

6. Terri Adams-Fuller. "We Can Overcome Our Biases, Racial and Otherwise, by First Becoming Aware of Them." *Quartz*, 19 June 2015. qz.com. Accessed 19 Sept. 2018.

7. Linda Tropp and Rachel Godsil. "Overcoming Implicit Bias and Racial Anxiety." *Psychology Today*, 23 Jan. 2015. psychologytoday.com. Accessed 19 Sept. 2018.

8. Adams-Fuller, "We Can Overcome Our Biases, Racial and Otherwise, by First Becoming Aware of Them."

INDEX

ABOUT THE AUTHORS

DUCHESS HARRIS, JD, PHD

Professor Harris is the chair of the American Studies department at Macalester College and curator of the Duchess Harris Collection of ABDO books. She is the author and coauthor of recently released ABDO books including *Hidden Human Computers: The Black Women of NASA*, *Black Lives Matter*, and *Race and Policing*.

Before working with ABDO, she authored several other books on the topics of race, culture, and American history. She served as an associate editor for *Litigation News*, the American Bar Association Section of Litigation's quarterly flagship publication, and was the first editor in chief of *Law Raza*, an interactive online journal covering race and the law, published at William Mitchell College of Law. She has earned a PhD in American Studies from the University of Minnesota and a JD from William Mitchell College of Law.

CARLA MOONEY

Carla Mooney is a graduate of the University of Pennsylvania. Today, she writes for young people and is the author of many books for young adults and children. Mooney enjoys learning about social issues and making the world a more inclusive place for all people.